AF007367

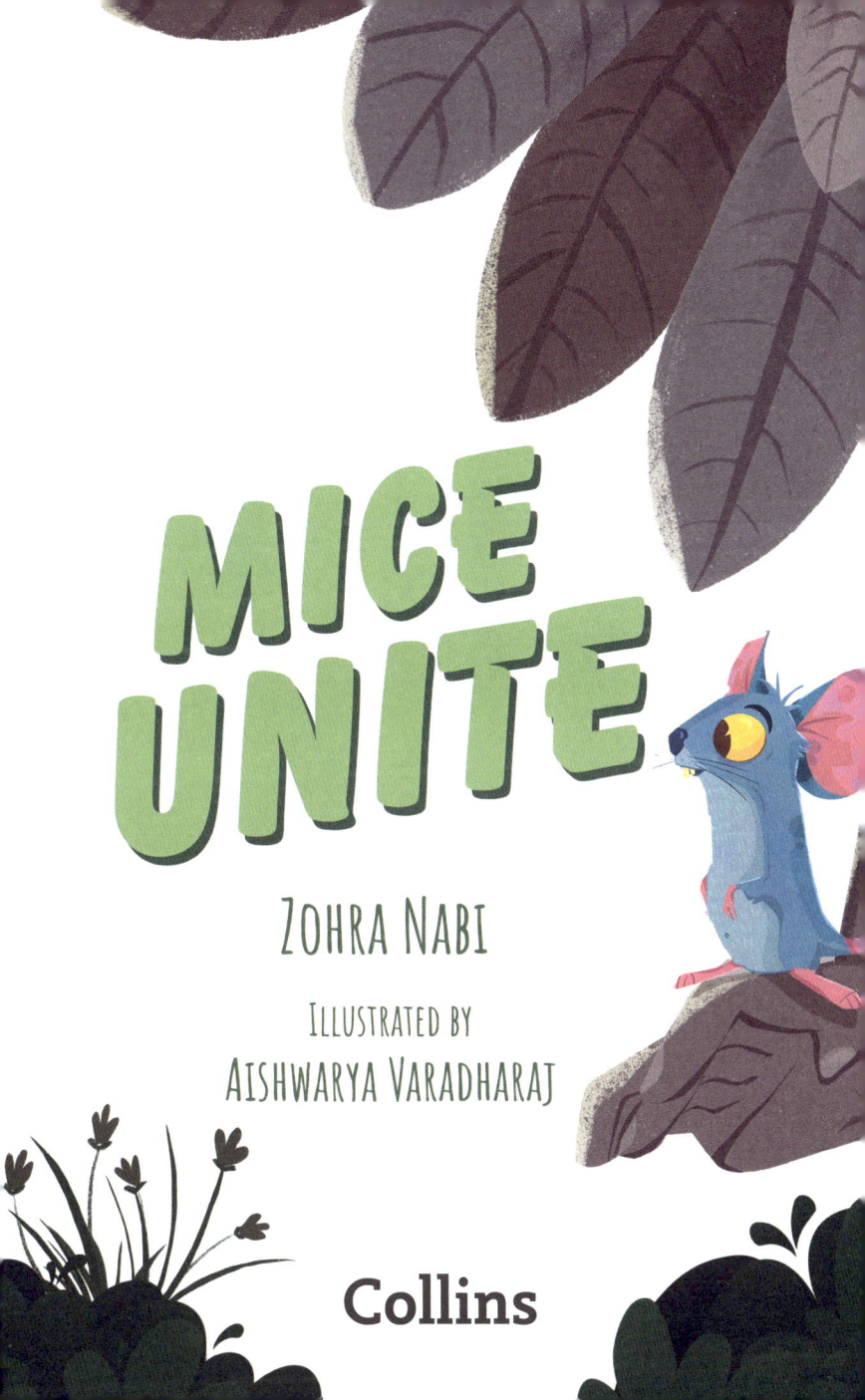

MICE UNITE

Zohra Nabi

Illustrated by
Aishwarya Varadharaj

Collins

Contents

Chapter 1 7
Bonus: Guide to Highgate Cemetery 22
Chapter 2 25
Bonus: Survival guide for the outdoors ... 38
Chapter 3 41
Bonus: Floor plan of the house 54
Chapter 4 57
Bonus: Survival guide for the indoors 70
Chapter 5 73
Bonus: Field mouse vs house mouse 86
Chapter 6 89
Bonus: Saima's diary 104
About the author 106
About the illustrator 108
Book chat 110

Chapter 1

Caspar Tail never thought he would lead a revolution. But even before he was known throughout London as a fearless general of revolting rodents, he was quite an extraordinary mouse. For a start, he lived in one of the largest graveyards in London. It was overgrown with ivy and sprawling trees, and yet so important that people came from far and wide to visit it.

There were long avenues winding through the grounds, lined with mausoleums that looked like stone houses complete with pillars and doors. There were marble tombs the size of small cars, towers and spires which stretched up into the sky. There were tall statues of angels, their wings outspread and their hands lifted up. Sometimes Caspar liked to take a few berries and climb onto the angels' palms, nibbling the fruit and enjoying his view of the city.

Caspar could see so far – to where there were glass spires and an enormous white dome ten times the size of anything in his cemetery.

At night, when the gates were locked and he could be sure that no humans were about, Caspar would hop from headstone to headstone. He would leap through the air, twisting and pirouetting, before landing elegantly on a patch of moss.

Caspar had taught himself lots of words by listening to the conversations people had around the graveyard. He could even read some of the writing on the graves.

He was better at some words than others. *Beloved* came up a lot, as did *dearly missed*. Caspar knew all the relationships too – he knew which graves belonged to a *beloved sister*, and which were the resting place of a *dearly missed grandfather*.

He couldn't remember his own family, and sometimes he found himself seeking out the places where the graves all had the same surname. Some headstones were more unusual than others. There was an enormous lion, as well as a dog resting by one of the graves, which Caspar was fairly sure was made from stone – but he still tiptoed around it, because you could never be *too* sure.

The grave he liked best had an enormous stone head mounted on it.

The head had thick eyebrows and a long, bushy beard. Written on the grave were the words: *WORKERS OF ALL LANDS UNITE.* Caspar didn't really understand what it meant. He supposed that the people who visited the grave were people from all over the world, and by gathering there they were uniting. He thought the grave must be very important. Either way, there was a tasty patch of dandelions growing next to the plinth.

The day everything changed, there was a storm. The rain was thick and syrupy with London soot, and it fell so hard that it ricocheted off the stone tombs. Caspar hated rain. Luckily, he had sought shelter beneath a stone angel's wing the second the sky had darkened. There was a group of people huddled by a grave with a pot full of pens.

It was raining heavily, and the visitors had only brought one umbrella. They stood, a shivering, miserable mass. Some people were staring at their phones, others were peering up gloomily at the sky.

"Mummy, I'm *hungry*," one of the smaller humans complained.

One of the taller ones next to him sighed. "Hang on. I'm sure I've got something in here." She took a small sack off her shoulder. Setting it on the ground, she rummaged around inside. After a short while, she drew out a *whole apple* and presented it to the small human.

Caspar watched, fascinated. In all his six months of living, he had never seen anything so miraculous. That apple hadn't grown on a tree – it wasn't even the season for ripe apples! Instead, it had appeared like magic from the woman's bag.

What else could the bag create? More dandelions perhaps – or caterpillars? Caspar always had to race the robins for the juiciest, wriggliest caterpillars.

Perhaps with this magical sack, he would never have to race them again. Braving the rain, Caspar made a run for it, scurrying through the grass.

Caspar made a flying leap and jumped into the woman's bag just as she picked it back up off the ground.

Inside the bag, Caspar waited expectantly. It was confusing – full of wriggly things that looked like worms, but white and made of plastic. There was a book, and a waxy lip balm, both of which Caspar nibbled on patiently as he wondered how to conjure an apple for himself.

But then he heard a voice coming from outside. "The taxi's here – let's make a run for it!"

Suddenly, Caspar was being jostled back and forth, and he bounced from one side of the bag to the other. His tail was tangled up in the white plastic worms, and in his panic, he bit through one to be free of it, revealing long strings of metal.

Keep calm, he told himself.

It was a long way to the top of the bag – but he was Caspar Tail. He leapt into the air, reaching for the daylight. But it was hard to get a grip on the soft surface.

He fell back into the bag. Gritting his teeth, he leant back on his hind legs and propelled himself into the air, springing forwards and grasping onto the handle of the bag as tightly as he could.

There was a loud scream from a man.

"AARGH! A mouse! There's a mouse on your bag!" a woman shouted, pointing.

Caspar knew he was in danger. As more screams joined the first, he jumped down from the handles, moving as quickly as he could along the floor and through the feet of the people.

To his horror, he saw that he was in a strange, grey box that smelt of boots and petrol.

The people were trying to stamp on him, and Caspar had to dart back and forth to stop himself from being squashed beneath their feet.

"Open the door! Open the door!" someone cried.

There was a new, beeping sound, and then Caspar could see daylight! Joyfully, he leapt down past the rows of boots and out into the world.

Guide to Highgate Cemetery

The graveyard where Caspar Tail lives is very similar to Highgate Cemetery, in North London. Here are some facts about Highgate Cemetery.

A lot of the cemetery is left wild, to encourage lots of different kinds of wildlife, including creatures like Caspar!

Famous people buried there include Karl Marx (a philosopher), Christina Rossetti (a poet) and Douglas Adams (a writer).

There are lots of interesting statues! There is a man trying to push a boulder up a hill, a lion, a horse and a piano.

A dog statue guards the grave of Thomas Sayers, a Victorian boxer.

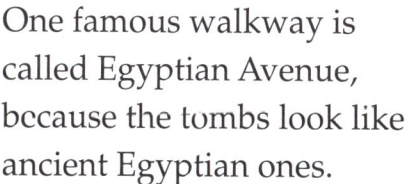

One famous walkway is called Egyptian Avenue, because the tombs look like ancient Egyptian ones.

Chapter 2

*W*HAM!

A car passed straight over Caspar's head. The smell of petrol was even stronger now, but it was mixed up with other strange, unfamiliar things. More cars drove over him, each one plunging him into terrifying darkness. But the daylight was strange too, not shaded with the green and yellow of trees, but brighter and starker. He needed to find shelter. Setting his head down, he charged ahead.

He didn't stop until he was inside a building. Even then he kept going. Under barriers, down steps. It was strange, the steps didn't behave like steps – they moved about, until Caspar felt dizzy. And every time he stopped to catch his breath, the same thing would happen.

"Mouse!"

"It's a mouse!"

"Ugh, how disgusting!"

Caspar thought this last comment was very unfair. Especially considering how disgusting humans were, looming like giants over everything.

He kept going, until he reached a walkway that stretched into a vast, gaping tunnel. Someone had painted a yellow line to mark the path, and Caspar followed it desperately.

Caspar's wits were finely tuned to the outside world. He could tell the difference between the scents of a dog fox and a vixen, and he knew by feel alone which berries were safe to eat and which were deadly poison.

But this place … every sense he had seemed to have exploded. Bright, white light flooded his eyes. The air was full of screeching, louder than any owl, louder than the mysterious metal boxes humans moved around in.

Caspar's bones were humming, his heart an angry buzz in his ribcage. Even that was nothing compared to the *smells*. Not fresh, outdoor smells like the ones in his cemetery.

There were wrappers, packets, crumpled cans on benches, empty styrofoam boxes smeared in sticky sauce on the floor.

Even as he lurked in the shadows, Caspar longed to eat and eat until he could eat no more.

But just then, he caught sight of something extraordinary. It was another mouse. She was impossibly small, her ears flat against her skull. Her tail – a mere stump. But she was undoubtedly one of his kind.

What was more, she was carrying a whole crisp in her mouth.

"Hey!" he called. "Hey – stop!"

The mouse paid no attention. She walked right past Caspar without so much as turning her head.

"HEY!" Caspar bellowed.

The mouse stopped. She blinked, twitching her nose.

"I'm awfully sorry. Were you trying to talk to me?" she said through her mouthful.

"Of course I was talking to you – can't you hear me?"

"What?" The mouse put a paw to her ear. "You'll have to speak up, I'm afraid. We're all deaf down here, because of the trains."

"Trains?" Caspar asked. But then the white light flashed again, and he heard the ear-splitting screech as something raced towards them from the tunnel.

Surely that had to be the trains – there couldn't be a louder sound in the world than that.

"Mind the gap!" a human voice blared out.

"I'm Max," said the crisp-carrying mouse. "You want to chat? You'll have to get on, I can't miss my train."

"Get on?" asked Caspar, appalled.

To his horror, Max took a running jump. She soared over the yellow line, landing *inside the train* itself.

"Come on," she said. "It's pretty much an empty carriage – but it'll be rush hour soon, and I wouldn't fancy your chances on the platform then."

Caspar didn't know what rush hour was, but he didn't like the sound of it. Taking a deep breath, he jumped, closing his eyes until he was safely inside what Max had called "the carriage".

The doors closed behind him, and suddenly they were moving, faster than Caspar had in the taxi. It was a strange place, the carriage.

There were two rows of benches facing each other, and windows that looked out onto blackness.

"That was a good jump," said Max, admiringly. "A lot of good mice have lost their tails to those closing doors. Including me." She displayed her stump, proudly. "You hungry?"

Caspar remembered his patch of dandelions sadly. "Starving!"

"All right. We can talk over dinner."

"Dinner" took place in the cracks between the seats of the carriage. It was a sumptuous three-course meal. There was half a crisp each followed by burger crumbs, finished off with the inside of a chocolate wrapper each.

Max talked all the while.

"I'm a Chewb mouse – that's what the humans call this place: the Chewb. Probably because there's so much good stuff to eat. You're welcome to join our gang, if you like. I'll look after you."

Caspar was tempted. But then he remembered Max's missing tail.

"No, thanks!" he said, as loudly as he could. "I'd rather get back to my graveyard, thank you!"

"Can't go back," said Max, seriously. "Not on the Chewb. All you can do is get off."

"Get off? Where?"

"Anywhere you like. If you want to live your life underground, stay here. If not – pick a bag, any bag, and ride it all the way home. Well, to *someone's* home, anyway.

Who knows, you might even end up in a house!"

"A house?" Caspar remembered the stone tombs. "You can't get *inside* a house!"

"Course you can," said Max, dreamily. "A house with a kitchen – apparently, there's all the food you could want, and a nice warm nest to live out your days. Me, I'm a hard Chewb mouse, and I belong to the platforms and the trains. But you seem like a nice kid.

Don't live your life underground – have an adventure. Climb into a bag and see where you end up."

At Max's words, Caspar felt a surge of courage. The carriage came to a juddering halt, and he took a deep breath. When the doors opened, more humans than he had ever seen before piled in, and all kinds of bags were set down on the floor.

Caspar scuttled along the floor of the carriage, wondering which bag to go for. A brown leather handbag? A shiny briefcase? And then he saw the ideal mode of transport. A green shopping bag, with a baguette sticking out between the handles. Perfect. He slipped in so quickly that not even Max could have seen quite where he went.

Survival guide for the outdoors

> I lived in a graveyard for a very long time – here are my tips for surviving outdoors!

Forage for food – insects are a great source of protein. Look for berries in winter and dandelions in spring.

Humans often leave litter – which is bad but sometimes tasty! Follow humans around when possible.

Keep out of the way of birds of prey!

Make sure you find a good shelter, where you'll be protected from rain and snow. A crack or crevice is a great place.

Chapter 3

It was very comfortable in the bag, and Caspar fell asleep amidst the folds of a purple jumper, with the scent of fresh bread in his nostrils. When he awoke, it was dark outside, but he knew immediately that he wasn't *in* the dark, with the owls and the insects that swarmed. He was warm and sheltered. He could hear a comforting thrum, like running water. And all around him he could smell food.

Not berries and insects, nor crisps. Something utterly new and completely delightful. When he got out, he saw immediately why Max had spoken of a *house* in such longing tones.

Everything was so much softer than the graveyard. Whatever he was walking on, it felt like how he imagined the clouds must feel. He crept forwards and immediately stumbled across an abandoned pea on the floor.

There was a table the height of a tombstone with a whole *bowl* of fruit on top. And, on a raised surface, a jar full of something Caspar thought were *biscuits*.

This must be the kitchen. The promised land. Caspar scaled the table leg as quickly as he could and got his paws on a banana with a split skin. Life, he thought, couldn't get better.

At that very moment, he knew he wasn't alone.

Every hair on his back stood on end; his heart whirred so fast that it sounded at the same pitch as his squeaks. It was the *smell*. Everything about it screamed danger.

Then he saw them. A pair of yellow eyes lit up in the dark.

Caspar didn't hesitate. He took a flying leap from the table, landing hard on his front paws, but not stopping, just running.

He was faster than water, faster than a falling stone. But the thing behind him was fast too; he could hear the scratch of its paws on the ground. It was making a sound in the back of its throat, the beginning of a growl that would open up a mouth to swallow him whole. He needed an escape, but he couldn't even smell the outside anymore.

So, he couldn't go outside. But could he go further *in*? Would a kitchen have something like a burrow, somewhere? He strained his eyes, moving so quickly all the while that it was hard to focus. But all he could see was unbroken white, and then strange tall machines he didn't understand. And then a gap! A gap in the wall, or the floor, it didn't matter.

Hardly daring to believe in it, he made a dive for the crack. It was a hole as small as a pea, but he squeezed himself through. As he went down, he felt the swipe of the creature's claws on his tail. He saw a yellow eye again, pressed up against the crack. But there was nothing it could do. Whatever it was, it was far too large to get through.

His heartbeat slowing, Caspar looked around. The thrum he had heard before was louder here – he was somewhere behind the wall between the machines, in the belly of the house. He looked around. Perhaps it wouldn't be so bad to stay here, in the space behind the wall. He could venture out to the kitchen whenever the coast was clear and forage as much as he liked.

But homesickness for his old life in the graveyard overwhelmed him, and he felt as though his longing would burst out of him.

He nibbled on the wall, wishing he had never had the idea of climbing into bags.

"Psst!"

Caspar looked around. He wasn't sure he could take any more danger.

"*Psst!*"

"Whatever you are, just come out," said Caspar, trying to sound braver than he felt. "I bet I can take you."

"I bet you could," came the gloomy *squeak* from the shadows.

To Caspar's relief, it was another mouse that emerged. But a scrawnier, greasier looking mouse he didn't think he had ever seen. He looked more frightened of Caspar than Caspar had been of the Chewb and the creature combined.

"I knew it was another mouse!" said the scrawny mouse, his nose twitching. "We smelt you hours ago. You can't have this patch, you know – it's ours! I'll fight you for it!"

The other mouse raised his fists half-heartedly.

Caspar tried not to roll his eyes. "You don't seem to be getting much out of your 'patch'," he said instead. "You look like you haven't eaten in weeks."

The other mouse bristled. "Haven't you met that *thing* outside? You try scavenging for crumbs with it on the prowl."

"But it can't be there all the time. Couldn't you go out then?" asked Caspar.

The other mouse sighed. "It's easiest if I just take you to her. She's much better at explaining than I am."

"Take me to who?"

"The Mousetriarch. She'll explain it best. I'm Jammy Crumb the Third, by the way. Nice to meet you."

"Thanks. It's Caspar. Caspar Tail."

Jammy led Caspar further into the house.

They went past hot copper pipes and pieces of fluffy yellow wool. These led a trail to the most enormous nest Caspar had ever seen. There must have been hundreds of mice, shivering together.

"Granny!" Jammy called. "I've brought him to see you. The new mouse!" He turned to Caspar. "This is Mrs Granary Toast Crumb: the Mousetriarch. My twelve-times great-grandmother. She's ancient – nearly four years old – and wiser than all of us put together."

A mouse with the size and appearance of a wizened walnut emerged from the middle of the nest.

"Greetings, newcomer," she said, in regal tones.

Caspar sensed he should be very polite.

"Greetings, Mrs Crumb."

"Oh, call me Granny. All the rest of them do. Can you believe when I first brought my children here, there was enough food to feed thousands of mice? Now, we exist on so little."

She peered at Caspar. "There's not much, young man – but what we have, we'll share."

"Why has it got so much worse?" asked Caspar.

Granny sighed. "New humans moved in last year. They're so *clean*; you're lucky if you can find one crumb. Not to mention their awful cat, prowling about. If things don't change soon, then we'll all waste away down here."

Floor plan of the house

54

Chapter 4

Caspar wrinkled his nose. "I don't understand why you can't get food. I could smell so much food upstairs."

"Oh, there's lots of food." Jammy's eyes went wide as saucers. "There's a massive box called the *fridge*, and another few called *cupboards* and they're full of as much food as you can eat. But if we go out in the open – " He shuddered. "The cat will get us. Or the big one will put down *traps*."

"They're evil," another mouse spoke up. "You think you're getting a nice bit of cheese or peanut butter, and then – *WHAM!*" He leapt forwards at Caspar, who didn't flinch. "They're ruthless, humans. All we can do is stay out of their way."

Caspar looked around at the group. "Is this really how you want to live the rest of your lives? Cowering beneath the floorboards, eating the scraps that humans leave behind?"

"What other choice do we have?" asked Jammy.

"I'll tell you what choice you have," said Caspar. "You can choose to not give up! Why should the humans get all the nice things, just because they're bigger than us? They might have invented bags and fridges – but we've been around just as long as they have, and this is our world too. They need to learn to share it with us! We have rights."

Some of the mice looked interested in his speech – more of them, however, looked doubtful.

"Why would humans ever share with us?" asked Granny.

"Because we can make them," said Caspar, firmly. "Don't you know how scared of us they are? I caused chaos today as one mouse – what can we do as hundreds? We need to … to – " He remembered the words carved on the bushy-bearded statue in the graveyard.

WORKERS OF ALL LANDS UNITE

"We need to unite! To all come together to make a difference. What have we got to lose?" He registered a look of horror on Jammy's face, but everyone else looked excited. A plan was forming.

"Where do we start?" asked Granny.

"First the traps," he said. "Then the cat. Then – the kitchen is ours."

They started on the traps the next morning. Caspar was reliably informed that the cat would be out chasing birds in the garden. In the daylight, the kitchen did look like a wonderful haven. There were cheerful rainbow tiles, and pictures on the fridge, although those were mostly of the cat. Caspar regarded the image of his foe scornfully.

Then he turned his attentions to the traps. They really were very nasty.

One was baited with a smear of peanut butter, the other with a hunk of cheese, and the smallest mis-step would leave a mouse in a very nasty position indeed.

"The key to these traps," he announced to the mice surrounding him, "is *balance*. Mice are naturally good at acrobatics. Watch and learn."

Putting all of his gravestone-hopping to good use, Caspar balanced on his two front paws and did a neat handstand.

With great elegance, Caspar licked the peanut butter in the trap. Then, leaning back on his hind legs, he took a flying leap and snatched the cheese from the second trap midair.

"You see?" he said importantly. "All we have to do is use our natural skills, and these traps should pose no problems for us. You try."

Reluctantly at first, and then with increasing delight, the assembly of mice began to leap through the air, taking it in turns to scrape the peanut butter off the trap.

The air filled with squeaks as the mice realised the future possibilities. Traps held no fear for them now.

Unfortunately for them, the squeaks reached such a deafening volume that they could be heard from outside.

There was the sound of a rusty hinge, and a pair of yellow eyes emerged from the cat flap.

Most of the mice shrank back in horror – but Caspar lifted his chin. In the daylight, this creature was barely the size of a fox, and so much smaller than a dog. "Don't be afraid!" he said. "Remember what I told you: we're only small if we stand alone."

Most of the mice had retreated to the crack in the kitchen walls, and Caspar made as though he was going to follow them. Thinking Caspar was retreating, the cat's eyes lit up, and he began a nonchalant prowl towards the group of cowering mice.

"On the count of three," Caspar announced. "One, two … three!"

He took another death-defying leap and landed squarely on the cat's nose.

The cat gave a yowl of astonishment, trying with all his might to shake Caspar off, forgetting his plan to eat him. Encouraged by Caspar's recklessness, the other mice joined him, jumping up onto various parts of the cat and sinking their teeth into his side.

The cat was genuinely terrified now, howling in pain and wriggling from side to side to shake off the mice.

"We're winning the fight!" Caspar yelled. "We're united! And mice united will never be defeated!"

There was a chorus of rallying squeaks.

The mouse attack had left the cat severely shaken. It fled through its cat flap and perched on the shed roof, a haunted look in its eyes. Meanwhile, the mice had free rein of the kitchen.

How to gain access to the inner delights of the fridge remained a mystery to them, but one of the cupboards had been left slightly ajar.

The mice feasted on spilt golden syrup and granola from an open box.

The syrup made Caspar feel incredibly giddy. He swung across the kitchen on the cord of a blind, on top of the world.

Then Jammy scurried out from his lookout post by the kitchen door. "The humans!" he yelled. "They're back!"

Sure enough, there was the sound of a key turning in the lock.

Every single mouse, except Caspar, fled back to the cracks in the walls and holes in the floorboards as quickly as possible.

"Caspar, what are you doing?" Jammy called. "Get back here, now!"

Caspar, still dizzy with power, lingered. He wanted to see the humans in their natural habitat – they always seemed so out of place in the graveyard.

Survival guide for the indoors

After a few weeks spent indoors, I feel confident that I know all the tricks for making it indoors as a mouse.

If something looks too good to be true, it's probably a trap.

Find a place you won't be in the way – behind the washing machine is warm and usually has easy access to the kitchen!

Sniff around after someone's cooked dinner; there will usually be a few crumbs! Wait until the humans have gone to bed, though …

Watch out for cats. They smell awful, so you'll have plenty of warning.

CHAPTER 5

The two humans who entered the kitchen looked very similar – perhaps a *beloved mother* and a *much-missed daughter*, like on the headstones. Both had brown skin, and black, straight hair. They were making a lot of noise, even for humans.

"Now I want you going straight to your room, Saima," the taller one said, sternly. "You've got homework to do."

"But Mum, I need to practise my recorder first," Saima said patiently.

She was very small and had an intelligent look in her eyes. "I can't possibly do that in my bedroom."

As they bickered, Caspar crept closer. He felt something like homesickness, seeing how close they were. How much love there was between them, even as they disagreed. He found himself staring.

At which point, the older human locked eyes with him, and let out an eardrum-bursting yell. "A mouse! A mouse on the kitchen counter!"

Embarrassed, Caspar jumped down. But Mum snatched a broom and brought it crashing down on the spot where he had just been. At the same time, she jumped on a chair.

Luckily, Caspar was fast, and he was safely back in the hole before the broom could cause any serious damage. Still, he burnt with anger.

"Are you all right?" asked Jammy.

"No, I'm not all right," said Caspar. "And I won't be, until the injustices of the kitchen are righted. It's not enough to fool the traps or fight the cat. We have to overcome the humans themselves."

Outside, Caspar could hear Saima speaking soothingly. "There, it's gone now, Mum. Are you all right?"

"No, I'm not." Mum's voice was shaky. "That mouse was right by where I make your packed lunches – and it's probably carrying all kinds of germs! Tomorrow I'm calling out Pest Control. They'll get rid of the problem."

"Get rid of the problem?" one of the other mice asked, worriedly. "What does that mean?"

"It's an empty threat," said Caspar, airily. "Don't pay any attention."

But the next day, when Caspar woke up, there was something new waiting for them by the kitchen cupboards. It looked like blue grains of rice.

"Wow!" Jammy breathed. "That smells amazing!"

But Caspar looked at the new blue food with narrowed eyes. He remembered when there had been a lot of slugs in the graveyard last year, more than he could eat, and the gardeners had put some strange blue things in the soil. You didn't see many slugs, after that.

"Don't eat it," he said. "There's something funny about the blue pellets: spread the word."

As Jammy obeyed, Caspar looked out into the hallway with suspicious eyes. If the humans wanted a battle, they had found one.

After the incident with the pellets, none of the mice held back. They were everywhere, finding their way into kitchen cupboards, into the fruit bowl, even into Saima's packed lunch. Once they even dared venture into the sitting room, where Mum and Saima were watching television.

The screams drowned out the show they were watching for quite some time. All the screams were Mum's. Sometimes Saima looked almost curiously at Caspar, as though she would like to get to know him. But he didn't have time to think about that. He was fighting a battle, and he was winning. Nothing in the house was off limits. Only one last human creation remained for Caspar to conquer.

This was the fridge, of course. The home of all manner of food, where mice could feast for thousands of years and be content.

"We can't do it," said Jammy, every night. "It's impossible. The door is too heavy."

"Nothing's impossible for us," said Caspar. "Not for the united mice."

In the end, just as before, a combination of acrobatics and Caspar's intelligence won the day.

One night, after preparing himself all day, he put a plan into motion. He began by swinging from his favourite blind cord and spinning sharply when he reached the fridge door, looping the string around the handle. It was perfectly taut, strained to its absolute limit.

"Now!" Caspar called. At his word, ten mice jumped onto the cord, clinging on with their teeth. The tension was enough to pull at the fridge door, for it to strain …

And then open! Just a crack, but a crack was all they needed. The fridge was conquered. The mice surged joyfully from their hideout and scaled the former fortress.

All the food they wanted was theirs – vegetables, yoghurt, even *eggs*. Caspar's mouth watered at the thought of eggs.

Unfortunately, what he hadn't realised was that when the fridge door was left open, a powerful alarm sounded.

It was irritating at first, but then it became unbearable as it got louder. Loud enough to wake Mum, who came into the kitchen in a pink dressing gown, rubbing her eyes.

At the sight of the mice, her mouth fell open. At first, she just looked at them all, wide-eyed. Then she began to scream, so loudly that Caspar's ears hurt. The mice began to scramble.

They ran into each other in panic as they attempted to escape the fridge.

"Mum!" Caspar heard Saima call out. "What's wrong?"

"That's it!" Mum shrieked. "I've had it with these wretched rodents. We're getting builders round – decorators, plasterers, anyone who can tell us how to seal these mice up in the wall, where they belong!"

Caspar couldn't help but worry when he heard Mum's words. *Seal them up in the wall?*

They'd starve – there was hardly any food back there.

And things only got worse when Caspar returned to the nest. Everyone turned on him in a fury.

"Now you've done it," Granny squeaked, her voice high-pitched with anger. "Do you know what builders do? They come in with hammers and drills, and our lovely house becomes a place of noises and cold.

And do you know who comes with the cold? *Rats*, that's who! There's nothing a rat likes better than a tasty mouse as a snack. Just look outside!"

Caspar obeyed Granny, and his heart sank. Waiting outside he could see a whole gang of shadowy, large figures with long tails. Rats! They looked just as united as the mice.

Field mouse vs house mouse

Field mouse

- has strong back feet, great for jumping
- loves to eat nuts, berries and insects
- has larger ears and eyes
- is cautious but adventurous
- can fit in a hole the size of an HB pencil

HOUSE MOUSE

- has a thick, scaly tail to help it balance

- will eat anything but loves sugar

- is bold in travelling through a house, but ready to run away at the first sign of danger

- can fit in a hole the size of an HB pencil

Chapter 6

"All right," said Caspar, "I'll fix the problem of the builders, don't worry. I've fixed things before; I can fix them again."

"You'd better," said Granny. "Or we'll all be flying the nest – and let me tell you, you'll be the first to pack your bags."

Caspar thought long and hard about how he could save the mice from certain peril. It didn't help that everyone in the house was looking at him very accusingly.

It didn't help, either, that the group of shadowy figures with long tails was growing closer by the day, it seemed.

Mum had the builders around every day, and they'd been making lots of comments about replacing floorboards and knocking out walls. Caspar didn't like the sound of that at all.

He thought about how the mice had all banded together. And they had got everything they wanted! But maybe that wasn't the point.

Because it wasn't enough to get a little bit more cheese one week or cleverly avoid a trap the next week. Uniting needed to make life better for all mice, for a long time. And maybe not just mice. Maybe it needed to make *everyone's* life a bit better, at least as far as it could. If Caspar came up with a solution, it would have to be *with* the humans if it was going to last.

They couldn't work with Mum – you couldn't ask someone nicely not to have builders around when they screamed every time they saw you. But Saima … perhaps … Maybe Caspar could talk to Saima.

She did her homework at the kitchen table. As soon as her mum was on a work call, Caspar scaled the kitchen leg and went up to her slowly, twitching his nose. Saima's eyes widened, but she didn't scream.

He squeaked a question. "Do you understand me?"

"Hello," she breathed. "You're a very sweet little mouse."

Caspar nodded. Already he saw the flaw in his plan – he could understand her perfectly, but she couldn't understand him.

And then he saw the answer. He remembered the grave with the pens by it – that was because the person buried there was a writer. You could use pens to write, and writing is another way to communicate!

Caspar grabbed a pen, prising the lid off with his teeth and then holding the pen in his mouth and front paws. From the corner of his eye, he saw Saima lean forwards and watch him, fascinated.

"That's – that's a letter shape. Are you? No! Are you … *writing*?"

Very carefully, he began to make the shape of the only word he knew which he felt had enough power to make a human pay attention.

"You are! You're writing! How incredible." She came over and peered at his scrawled letters. "U-N-I-T-E – unite. Who? You want *us* to unite? Why?"

Caspar gave a squeak, and drew out the letter B.

"B … B … Err, the builders?!" cried Saima. "I don't want them to come either. But what can we do? So long as there are mice here, Mum won't feel relaxed in her own home."

It was funny – a mouse is so much smaller than a human. *Why are so many humans so scared?* Caspar thought, and at that moment his eyes and Saima's met, and the same light inside them sparked and landed on an idea.

"So," said Saima. "We need to convince Mum that she *doesn't* have mice anymore."

She got a book out of her bag and showed it to Caspar. As she turned the pages, Caspar knew they had the right strategy.

The next day, Caspar and Saima took their positions. Saima prepared a cup of tea for her mum, while Caspar stood at the head of hundreds of mice, poised by their crack in the kitchen wall.

"This had better work," Granny muttered to Caspar, who gulped.

Saima stepped forwards, ready to play her part. "Mum, I have a surprise for you!" she announced. "I can rid our home of mice."

Mum raised an eyebrow. "And how do you plan on doing that?"

"Simple – with *music*. Mice hate high, discordant notes. If I play my recorder, they're bound to leave." She drew out her instrument with a beam.

Mum laughed and placed a kiss on Saima's head. "All right, duckling. Give it a try."

"And you promise, if it works, there won't be any builders?"

"I promise."

With a grin, Saima played her recorder, making screechy, breathy sounds that would disgrace a pelican with a sore throat. But on cue, Caspar went charging out. And to his very great relief, all the mice behind him came out as well – some grumbling, but all still trusting he could lead them in the right direction.

Which, on that particular occasion, was out through the cat flap.

"Look at them go!" Saima crowed, in between puffs on her recorder. "There must be at least twenty, all leaving because of the music – and we can seal up the cat flap once they're gone!

Caspar suppressed a grin, as he led his troupe of mice out into the garden – and then straight up the wall and onto Saima's windowsill. There she had made several old shoe boxes into a highly comfortable mouse nest. There was fluffy insulation, and granola from the kitchen cupboard.

"Right, then," said Caspar. "I'm to oversee the mouse evacuation. Saima has agreed to look after some of you in here and treat you as pets – she will build a den in the garden which will house a good number of mice. The rest will be taken to sanctuaries at her school or in local parks. Some will be taken to the local graveyard, where I can assure you there is plentiful food for all."

"What about you?" asked Jammy, who had followed Caspar straight away. "What will you do?"

Caspar turned to face the direction of the wind. Clearing out the mice would take a long time, of course, even with Saima's help. But after that? He wouldn't go back to the graveyard. What was it the Chewb mouse had said? You couldn't go back, only get off. And Caspar thought he had quite the journey ahead of him yet.

Saima's diary

<u>Monday</u>

This week I'm having a scary time with Mum. She saw a mouse and screamed and jumped on a chair. I don't like it when Mum screams.

<u>Tuesday</u>

Mice got into the cupboards and ate all my cereal, but that's OK because I don't like cereal with raisins in. Mum says she is at her limit, and she tried to put bad medicine down for the mice, but none of them ate it and I was glad.

Thursday

Great news! I talked to the Head Mouse who wanted us all to unite, and we have made a plan. I am practising my recorder in preparation.

Friday

Mum is very happy the mice have gone, although she says she doesn't know what to think. I now have some lovely pet mice in a cardboard box in my room. I feed them the cereal now.

About the author

What made you think of this story?

Last year our flat had a mouse infestation. We couldn't go into the kitchen at night without seeing a mouse. My flatmate and I tried everything to get rid of them and never caught one. We thought maybe they'd come in from the garden, and it made me wonder – what if just one garden mouse had come in and started a revolution of the house mice?

Zohra Nabi

Was it fun to write from the perspective of a mouse?

It was therapeutic! I was very scared of mice and found it difficult to sleep while they were in our flat. Imagining a story from the perspective of a mouse trying to make his way in the world made them seem less scary. I'm still crossing all my fingers they don't return this winter, though. Caspar was fun to write about, but sharing a kitchen with him was exhausting.

How do you come up with your characters? Are they based on anyone you know?

I think there's something quite toddler-like about Caspar that I observed from looking after my little cousin – something bold, cheeky and bossy; he's a mouse who wants to get his way whenever he can, but who is also learning that other people have feelings too. Saima's mum is definitely me. Some of the screams I let out last year when I saw a mouse could be heard for miles!

How do you know if an idea is going to be a good story?
I think it's when that idea meets another idea, and then the chain reaction of ideas just keeps going until you've found your way to a story with a beginning, middle and end. It's a really fun, fizzy feeling that I love – it's very addictive!

Do you have a favourite character in this book?
I have a soft spot for Granary 'Granny' Toast Crumb. When we had mice, lots of people shared their mouse stories with us. A friend told me they had mice for so long, they found an elderly one with a white streak of fur! I had to put her into the story.

Did you have to research Highgate Cemetery?
I live in London, fairly close to Highgate Cemetery, but I still relied a lot on their website to see all the famous attractions. I wandered around Abney Park Graveyard in Stoke Newington, too. And of course, people who use the night tube in London have seen the famous tube mice! I love writing about London, it's my favourite place in the world.

What's your favourite part of the book and illustration?
I think my favourite part is Caspar being on the tube with Max – it was such a fun scene to write! Aishwarya has done such a gorgeous job with the illustrations, but I think my favourite has to be Caspar jumping over the trap – it's so fun, and full of life!

What do you hope readers take away from this book?
Mice infestations are horrible, but at the end of the day mice just want to get by in the world, the same as humans! I hope that makes them less scary to people like me.

About the illustrator

Did you always want to be an illustrator?

Not exactly! I began with architecture, which involved lots of sketches, designing, and creativity. But the more I illustrated, the more I fell in love with telling stories through art, until I couldn't imagine doing anything else.

Aishwarya Varadharaj

How did you get into illustrating?

It started out as a fun extra while I worked as an architect. I'd spend my evenings and weekends doing small commissions for friends and family. Things snowballed from there, and soon enough, illustrating became my main job. I made it official in 2021.

Do you use pens and paints or work digitally?

I adored working with traditional pens and paints during college. Nowadays, I mostly illustrate digitally on my iPad. It's clean, flexible, and I can endlessly experiment without worrying about spilling paint everywhere!

What was your favourite scene to illustrate?

The spread where Saima plays the recorder and all the mice sneak out through the door was pure joy to sketch! The movement, the mischief, the composition … It all came together beautifully.

What was the most challenging thing about illustrating this book?
Definitely imagining the world from Caspar's tiny mouse perspective! Turning everyday London into whimsical adventures, and capturing each chapter's unique mood required a ton of creativity and many lots of thinking. But totally worth it!

Did you do lots of research for scenes set in London?
Oh, loads! I've never been to London (yet!), but I virtually toured everything: streets, tube stations, cosy interiors, even cemeteries. Honestly, at this point, I'm practically qualified to give London sightseeing tips!

Which character did you identify with the most?
Saima, without a doubt. I was a dreamy kid, always imagining conversations with animals, and I was obsessed with music. Her gentle curiosity and wonder felt like a snapshot of my own childhood.

Which character was the most fun to draw?
There's something irresistibly charming about drawing Caspar, a mouse who has big adventures and even bigger emotions. Drawing all his adorable poses was genuinely delightful.

Have you ever had a pet?
Briefly, yes; a stray cat during my college days. Sadly, mum's allergies meant that our time together was short-lived. I still miss that little bundle of chaotic fur!

Would you like to communicate with animals?
Absolutely! Can you imagine the stories animals could tell?

Book chat

What was your favourite part of this book?

Do any of the characters change from the beginning of the story to the end? How?

Would you prefer to be an indoors or an outdoors mouse? Why?

What do you think Caspar learned about people and Saima learned about mice?

What do you think happens next in the story?

If you had to think of a new title for this book, what would you choose?

Do you have a favourite character in the book? If so, who and why?

If you could ask the author any question, what would you ask?

Book challenge:

Draw a picture of Caspar's next home.

Published by Collins
An imprint of HarperCollins*Publishers*

The News Building
1 London Bridge Street
London
SE1 9GF
UK

Macken House
39/40 Mayor Street Upper
Dublin 1
D01 C9W8
Ireland

Text © Zohra Nabi 2025
Illustrations and design © HarperCollins*Publishers* Limited 2025

10 9 8 7 6 5 4 3 2 1

ISBN 978-0-00-876798-3

All rights reserved. No part of this publication may be reproduced, stored in a retrieval system, or transmitted in any form by any means, electronic, mechanical, photocopying, recording or otherwise, without the prior written permission of the Publisher or a licence permitting restricted copying in the United Kingdom issued by the Copyright Licensing Agency Ltd, 5th Floor, Shackleton House, 4 Battle Bridge Lane, London SE1 2HX.

Without limiting the exclusive rights of any author, contributor or the publisher of this publication, any unauthorised use of this publication to train generative artificial intelligence (AI) technologies is expressly prohibited. HarperCollins also exercise their rights under Article 4(3) of the Digital Single Market Directive 2019/790 and expressly reserve this publication from the text and data mining exception.

British Library Cataloguing-in-Publication Data
A catalogue record for this publication is available from the British Library.

Download the teaching notes and word cards to accompany this book at:
http://littlewandle.org.uk/signupfluency/

Get the latest Collins Big Cat news at
collins.co.uk/collinsbigcat

Author: Zohra Nabi
Illustrator: Aishwarya Varadharaj (The Bright Agency)
Publisher: Laura White
Commissioning editor and product manager: Caroline Green
Series editor: Charlotte Raby
Development editor: Catherine Baker
Project manager: Emily Hooton
Copyeditor: Sally Byford
Proofreader: Catherine Dakin
Cover designer: Sarah Finan
Typesetter: 2Hoots Publishing Services Ltd
Production controller: Sophie Waeland

Printed in the UK.

MIX
Paper | Supporting responsible forestry
FSC™ C007454

This book contains FSC™ certified paper and other controlled sources to ensure responsible forest management.

For more information visit: www.harpercollins.co.uk/green

Made with responsibly sourced paper and vegetable ink

Scan to see how we are reducing our environmental impact.

Acknowledgements
The publishers gratefully acknowledge the permission granted to reproduce the copyright material in this book. Every effort has been made to trace copyright holders and to obtain their permission for the use of copyright material. The publishers will gladly receive any information enabling them to rectify any error or omission at the first opportunity.

p86 Rudmer Zwerver/Shutterstock, p87 Szasz-Fabian Jozsef/Shutterstock.